D1305247

Countries of the World

England

by Kathleen W. Deady

Consultant:
Neal R. McCrillis, Ph.D.
Mildred Miller Fort Distinguished Chair of International Education
Associate Professor of History
Columbus State University

Bridgestone Books
an imprint of Capstone Press
Mankato, Minnesota

Bridgestone Books are published by Capstone Press
151 Good Counsel Drive, P.O. Box 669, Mankato, Minnesota 56002
http://www.capstone-press.com

Library of Congress Cataloging-in-Publication Data
Deady, Kathleen W.
    England/by Kathleen W. Deady.
    p. cm.—(Countries of the world)
    Includes bibliographical references and index.
    Summary: Discusses the history, landscape, people, animals, and culture of the country
of England.
    ISBN 0-7368-0627-X
    1. England—Juvenile literature. [1. England.] I. Title. II. Countries of the world
(Mankato, Minn.)
DA27.5 .D4 2001
942—dc21   00-024190

Editorial Credits

Tom Adamson, editor; Timothy Halldin, designer; Heidi Schoof and Kimberly Danger,
    photo researchers

Photo Credits

Index Stock Imagery, 5 (bottom)
Kay Shaw, 6
Photri-Microstock, 12
Shaffer Photography/James L. Shaffer, 10
StockHaus Limited, 5 (top)
Trip/J. Okwesa, cover; R. Bamber, 14; D. McGill, 16; M. Thornton, 18; H. Rogers, 20
Visuals Unlimited/Bud Nielsen, 8

1 2 3 4 5 6 06 05 04 03 02 01

Table of Contents

Fast Facts

Name: England

Capital: London

Population: More than 49 million

Language: English

Religion: Mostly Christian

Size: 50,333 square miles
(130,362 square kilometers)
*England is a little smaller than the
U.S. state of Alabama.*

Crops: Barley, wheat, potatoes

Maps

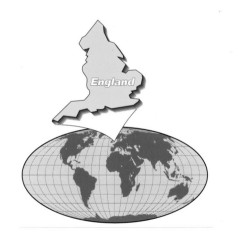

4

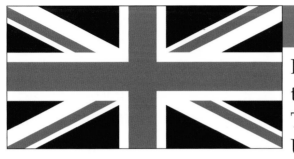

Flag

England is part of the United Kingdom. The Union Jack is the United Kingdom's official flag. The flag has three crosses that stand for three patron saints. The red cross of Saint George represents England. Saint Andrew's white diagonal cross is for Scotland. The red diagonal cross of Saint Patrick stands for Ireland. The flag became official in 1606. The government added Ireland's cross in 1801.

Currency

The unit of currency in England is the pound sterling. One hundred pence equal one pound.

In 2000, about 63 pence equaled 1 U.S. dollar. About 43 pence equaled 1 Canadian dollar.

The Land

England is on an island in western Europe. Scotland borders England to the north. Wales lies to the west. Together these three countries are called Great Britain. Great Britain and Northern Ireland make up the United Kingdom.

The North Sea borders England to the east. The English Channel lies to the south. These waters separate Great Britain from Europe's mainland. The Irish Sea and the Atlantic Ocean meet England's western shore.

England's landscape varies. The Pennine Mountains lie in the north. The western Lake District is a national forest. Deep valleys cross the Southwest Peninsula. Cliffs and beaches line the coast.

The Lowlands is an area of rich farmland in the middle of England. The Thames River flows through this region. The Thames is the longest river within England's borders.

England's Lowlands region contains rich farmland.

7

London

London is England's capital and largest city. More than 7 million people live there. London has many famous places.

The Thames River winds through London. This river is 210 miles (338 kilometers) long. Large bridges cross the Thames. The Tower Bridge is the most famous of these bridges.

Parliament stands next to the river. This government building is 950 feet (290 meters) long. Big Ben is a famous clock tower on the building. Westminster Abbey stands nearby. This famous church is more than 900 years old.

Several large parks in London give people a place to relax. People ride horses in Hyde Park and Kensington Gardens. They row boats on a narrow lake called the Serpentine. Many people also visit London Zoo in Regent's Park.

Workers completed the Tower Bridge in 1894.

Life at Home

Most English people live in or near cities. Many own their homes. Brick houses are common. The houses may be separate or joined together in a row. Many families plant gardens in their yards.

City centers are crowded. Some people live in tall apartment buildings. Others live in houses built in rows around factories.

Some English people live in the country. Their homes lie outside towns or in villages. Farming is still important in some areas of England. But modern farms need fewer workers. Most people from these areas drive into cities to work.

English families usually have one or two children. Both parents often work after the children are old enough to go to school. Families relax in the evening. They watch TV or visit with friends.

Many houses in England are joined together in rows.

Going to School

Education is important in England. Children must go to school from age 5 to 16. About 93 percent of students go to free state schools. The rest pay to go to private schools. In England, the best private schools are called public schools.

Students go to school Monday through Friday. A school year is called a form. Each form has three terms. Students have vacations at the middle and end of each term. Summer vacation lasts six weeks, from mid-July to September.

Children attend primary school from age 5 to 11. They then go on to secondary school until age 16. Students can prepare to attend a university or specialized training programs.

Students take tests at ages 7, 11, 14, and 16. The tests decide what kinds of classes students will take. Some students leave school at age 16 to work. Others stay two more years. They study for the test that will allow them to go to a university.

Most English children wear uniforms to school.

English Food

English food is simple. Beef, pork, and lamb are common meats. People often roast or boil potatoes. The English use fewer spices than other Europeans.

Names of dishes often tell what part of England they come from. A Cornish pasty is a flaky crust filled with meat, potatoes, and vegetables. Yorkshire pudding is a batter cake baked in meat fats. Lancaster hot pot is a lamb, oyster, and vegetable stew.

The English also enjoy other popular foods. Fish and chips is a favorite dish. Chips are French fries. Shepherd's pie is a casserole made of ground beef and mashed potatoes. The English eat biscuits and tea anytime.

Plum pudding is England's most famous dessert. A cook covers this dish with brandy and lights it on fire. The fire burns the sugar on the surface to make a sweet crust.

Cornish pasties are named after the county Cornwall.

Animals

People have cleared much of England's forests. But many wild animals still live in England. Red deer live in the Lake District. The western part of England has roe deer. Fallow deer live throughout England.

Other wild animals include wild ponies that live in the southwestern part of England. Otters are common on riverbanks. Different kinds of seals live along less populated coasts. Brown trout, salmon, and eel swim the rivers.

Some small animals live near people. Badgers are common on farms. Rabbits feed in gardens. Red foxes live near cities. People in London find hedgehogs in their bushes. Bats and field mice live throughout England.

People see many different birds in England. Small English robins live in gardens. Seagulls and hawks fly over coastal areas. Game birds include grouse, partridge, and pheasant.

Red deer have red-brown fur.

Sports and Games

English people play many sports. Soccer is the favorite national sport. The English call it football.

Rugby is another popular sport in England. Rugby is similar to American football. American football also is becoming popular in England.

Cricket is a traditional English game. The sport is at least 700 years old. Players use a ball and bat. The rules are complicated. A game of cricket can last several days.

Other popular sports include tennis and badminton. The world's biggest tennis tournament takes place at Wimbledon. National badminton championships are in Birmingham.

The English enjoy many other pastimes. Gardening is a favorite hobby. The English also enjoy golfing, fishing, and hunting. Many people relax in pubs after work. They play games such as dominoes, darts, and snooker. Snooker is a game similar to pool.

Cricket is a traditional English game.

Holidays and Celebrations

The English celebrate Guy Fawkes Day on November 5. In 1605, Guy Fawkes planned to blow up Parliament. People still celebrate that his plan failed. They light bonfires and shoot fireworks. They make dummies called "guys" and burn them on the bonfires.

Remembrance Day, or Poppy Day, is the closest Sunday to November 11. The English remember those who fought and died in World War I (1914–1918) and World War II (1939–1945). They wear paper poppies to show respect.

Many English families celebrate Christmas. They pull crackers before Christmas dinner. These small tubes are covered with bright colored paper twisted at the ends. People pull the ends to make the crackers explode open. Jokes and paper hats fall out. People wear the hats during dinner. Christmas dinner usually is roast turkey.

On Guy Fawkes Day, people burn "guys" on bonfires.

Hands On: Play Tiddlywinks

Tiddlywinks is a traditional English children's game. The game has two versions. It is easy to make and play.

What You Need

A flat surface
  (a smooth table or carpet)
Cardboard
Markers

2 large buttons
6 small buttons
Small paper cup
2 players

What You Do

1. Draw two straight lines on the cardboard 3 to 6 feet (1 to 2 meters) apart. These lines are the start and finish lines.
2. Each player has three small buttons and one large button. Press firmly on the edge of the small button with the large one. The small button will jump forward.
3. Take turns making a button jump. The first player to get three buttons past the finish line wins.

Version 2
On the cardboard, draw three or four circles one inside the other. Assign a certain number of points to each ring. A paper cup in the middle is the bull's-eye. Give the bull's-eye the highest score. Start at the outside ring. Take one shot for each button. The highest score wins.

Learn to Speak British English

The English names for some things are different from names in North America.

bobby	police officer	**jumper**	sweater
boot	car trunk	**lift**	elevator
cheers	thank you, goodbye	**loo**	toilet
cooker	stove	**lorry**	truck
crisps	potato chips	**nappy**	diaper
flat	apartment	**petrol**	gasoline

Words to Know

badminton (BAD-min-tuhn)—a game similar to tennis; players use rackets to hit a shuttlecock back and forth over a net.

brandy (BRAN-dee)—a strong alcoholic drink made from wine

patron saint (PAY-truhn SAYNT)—a saint who people believe looks after their country

peninsula (puh-NIN-suh-luh)—land surrounded by water on three sides

rugby (RUHG-bee)—a form of football played by two teams that kick, pass, or carry an oval ball

tournament (TUR-nuh-muhnt)—a series of games played to find out which team or player is best

traditional (truh-DISH-uh-nuhl)—using the styles, manners, and ways of the past

Read More

Burgan, Michael. *England*. A True Book. New York: Children's Press, 1999.

Enderlein, Cheryl L. *Christmas in England*. Christmas around the World. Mankato, Minn.: Hilltop Books, 1998.

Useful Addresses and Internet Sites

British Tourist Authority
111 Avenue Road, Suite 450
Toronto, ON M5R 3J8
Canada

Embassy of the United Kingdom
3100 Massachusetts Avenue NW
Washington, DC 20008

VisitBritain
http://www.visitbritain.com

The World Factbook 1999—United Kingdom
http://www.odci.gov/cia/publications/factbook/uk.html

Index